Discover Cyprus: A Comprehensive Travel Guide to the Jewel of the Mediterranean

Uncover the Rich History, Culture, and Natural Beauty of Cyprus, from Beaches to Mountains and Everything in Between

Patrakis Elena George

Table of Content

Chapter 1

Chapter 6

INTRODUCTION

Welcome to the stunning Mediterranean island of Cyprus! This beautiful destination is known for its crystal-clear waters, golden beaches, ancient history, and warm hospitality. With a rich cultural heritage and a vibrant modern lifestyle, Cyprus is a perfect blend of the old and the new. From picturesque villages to bustling cities, and from tranquil nature reserves to vibrant nightlife, there's something for everyone in Cyprus.

Whether you're an adventurer seeking outdoor thrills, a history buff eager to explore ancient ruins, a foodie looking to indulge in local delicacies, or simply someone seeking relaxation in the sun, Cyprus offers a plethora of experiences to suit your tastes.

In this comprehensive travel guide, we'll take you on a journey through the best that Cyprus has to offer. From top tourist attractions to hidden gems, and from practical tips to insider secrets, we've got you covered. So, grab your sunscreen and let's dive into the wonders of Cyprus!

Overview of Cyprus

Cyprus is a breathtakingly beautiful island situated in the eastern Mediterranean, just south of Turkey and west of Syria and Lebanon. Known as the "island of love" due to its mythological connections to the goddess Aphrodite, Cyprus boasts an incredibly rich history and culture that has been influenced by the many civilizations that have inhabited it over the centuries.

From the idyllic beaches of Ayia Napa and Protaras to the rugged peaks of the Troodos Mountains, Cyprus is a land of contrasts. The island is also home to ancient ruins, such as the Greco-Roman city of Kourion and the Tomb of the Kings, that are testament to its long and storied history. The capital city of Nicosia is a vibrant metropolis that blends old-world charm with modern-day amenities, while other cities such as Limassol and Paphos offer a more relaxed atmosphere that is perfect for those seeking a slower pace of life.

Cypriot cuisine is another highlight of the island, with its delicious mezze platters, fresh seafood, and sweet pastries tempting the taste buds of visitors from all over the world. And let's not forget about the world-famous Cypriot wine, which is produced in the scenic vineyards of the Troodos Mountains.

With its warm climate, friendly locals, and stunning natural beauty, Cyprus is a destination that truly has something for everyone. Whether you're seeking adventure, relaxation, or a mix of both, you're sure to find it on this charming island in the Mediterranean.

History of Cyprus

The history of Cyprus is as rich and varied as the island itself. Archaeological evidence suggests that humans have lived on the island for over 10,000 years, with the earliest inhabitants believed to have been the Neolithic farmers who arrived from the Middle East. Over the centuries, Cyprus has been ruled by various powers, including the Assyrians, Egyptians, Persians, and Romans.

One of the most significant periods in Cypriot history was the rule of the Venetians, who controlled the island from 1489 to 1571. During this time, the city of Nicosia was fortified with impressive walls and gates that still stand today, and many of the island's churches and monasteries were built. The Ottomans took control of Cyprus in 1571 and ruled for over three centuries, until the island was annexed by Britain in 1878.

The 20th century saw Cyprus become a battleground for various political factions, with tensions between the Greek and Turkish Cypriot communities leading to violence and eventually to the division of the island in 1974. Today, the

Republic of Cyprus occupies the southern two-thirds of the island, while the Turkish Republic of Northern Cyprus controls the northern third.

Despite the island's turbulent past, Cyprus has managed to preserve its unique cultural identity and heritage. Ancient ruins such as the Greco-Roman city of Salamis and the Tomb of the Kings are a testament to the island's rich history, while the vibrant traditions of Cypriot music, dance, and cuisine are still celebrated today.

As Cyprus continues to evolve and grow, its history remains an integral part of its identity, and a source of inspiration for those who visit this beautiful island in the Mediterranean.

Geography of Cyprus

Cyprus is the third-largest island in the Mediterranean, with a total area of around 9,251 square kilometers. The island is located in the eastern Mediterranean, south of Turkey and west of Syria and Lebanon. Cyprus is known for its stunning natural beauty, which is characterized by its rugged coastline, rolling hills, and picturesque mountains.

The island's highest peak is Mount Olympus, which stands at 1,952 meters above sea level and is located in the Troodos mountain range in the center of the island. The Troodos mountains are home to many scenic villages and are a popular destination for hiking and skiing. The highest point on the northern side of the island is the peak of the Kyrenia mountain range, which rises to a height of 1,024 meters.

Cyprus has a warm and sunny Mediterranean climate, with hot summers and mild winters. The island's coastline is dotted with numerous beaches and bays, ranging from the tourist hotspots of Ayia Napa and Protaras to more secluded stretches of sand such as Lara Bay and Fig Tree Bay.

In addition to its natural beauty, Cyprus is also known for its rich history and culture. The island has a long and storied past that is reflected in its many archaeological sites, ancient ruins, and historic landmarks. From the Roman amphitheater of Kourion to the medieval castle of Kolossi, Cyprus offers visitors a unique blend of natural wonders and cultural treasures.

Overall, the geography of Cyprus is diverse and striking, offering visitors a wealth of opportunities to explore and discover the island's many charms.

Culture and Tradition of Cyprus

The culture and traditions of Cyprus are as diverse and colorful as the island's landscape. The island has been inhabited by various civilizations throughout history, each leaving their mark on the culture and traditions of Cyprus. Here are some highlights of Cypriot culture and traditions:

Food: Cypriot cuisine is a delicious blend of Mediterranean and Middle Eastern flavors. The most famous Cypriot dish is probably the mezze, which is a collection of small dishes served as appetizers or as a main meal. Mezze can include dips, salads, grilled meats, and seafood. Other popular Cypriot dishes include souvla (grilled meat skewers), kleftiko (slow-cooked lamb), and moussaka.

Music and dance: Cypriot music is characterized by its use of traditional instruments such as the bouzouki, tzouras, and baglamas. Folk music and traditional dances are still an important part of Cypriot culture, with regional variations in both the music and dance styles.

Religion: The majority of Cypriots are Orthodox Christians, and the island is home to numerous historic churches and monasteries. Religious festivals, such as Easter and Christmas, are celebrated with great enthusiasm throughout the island.

- Language: The official languages of Cyprus are Greek and Turkish, reflecting the island's historical and political divisions. Many Cypriots are bilingual and speak both languages fluently.

- Hospitality: Cypriots are known for their warm and welcoming hospitality, and visitors to the island are often treated like family. It's not uncommon for locals to invite visitors into their homes for a meal or a drink, and a friendly conversation.

- Weddings: Weddings are a big part of Cypriot culture, and traditional weddings often involve elaborate ceremonies and celebrations that can last for several days. It's also customary for guests to bring money as a gift for the newlyweds.

Overall, the culture and traditions of Cyprus are a vibrant and colorful reflection of the island's history and diversity. Visitors to Cyprus can immerse themselves in this rich culture by trying the local cuisine, attending traditional festivals, and exploring the island's many historic landmarks.

CHAPTER 1

PLANNING YOUR TRIP TO CYPRUS

Planning a trip to Cyprus can be an exciting experience, and there are several things you should consider before embarking on your journey. Here are some tips to help you plan your trip to Cyprus:

- **Decide when to visit**: Cyprus enjoys a mild Mediterranean climate, with hot and dry summers and mild and wet winters. The best time to visit Cyprus depends on your preferences and what you want to do while you're there.

  If you're looking for a beach vacation, the best time to visit Cyprus is between June and September when the weather is warm and sunny, and the sea is perfect for swimming. The summer months are also the peak tourist season in Cyprus, so expect crowds and higher prices. If you want to avoid the crowds, consider going in May or October when the weather is still pleasant but the crowds have thinned out.

If you're interested in exploring the countryside and doing outdoor activities like hiking, the best time to visit Cyprus is in the spring (March to May) or autumn (September to November). During these months, the weather is cooler, and the landscapes are green and lush. You'll also avoid the scorching heat of the summer months.

If you're interested in experiencing traditional Cypriot festivals and cultural events, the best time to visit Cyprus is in the winter (December to February). During this time, you can enjoy events like the Christmas markets, the Limassol Carnival, and the Kataklysmos Festival, which celebrates the start of summer and includes water-based activities.

Overall, Cyprus is a year-round destination, and the best time to visit depends on your interests and what you want to do while you're there.

- **Choose your destinations**: Cyprus has a lot to offer, from beautiful beaches and ancient ruins to picturesque villages and scenic mountain ranges. Decide on the destinations you want to visit and plan your itinerary accordingly. Popular destinations include Nicosia, Limassol, Paphos, Larnaca, and Ayia Napa.

- **Book your accommodation**: Cyprus has a range of accommodation options, including luxury hotels, budget hotels, guesthouses, and holiday apartments. Book your accommodation in advance to check availability and get the best price .

- **Transportation:** Cyprus has a good public transportation system, including buses and taxis. If you prefer more flexibility, consider renting a car or a motorcycle to explore the island at your own pace. Just keep in mind that Cypriot roads can be narrow and winding, so it's important to drive safely and follow the rules of the road.

- **Pack accordingly:** Depending on the time of year you visit, you may need to pack accordingly. Cyprus is generally sunny and warm, so pack lightweight clothing, sunscreen, and a hat. If you plan to hike or explore the mountains, bring appropriate footwear and warm clothing.

- **Learn a few basic phrases:** While English is widely spoken in Cyprus, it's always helpful to learn a few basic phrases in Greek or Turkish, depending on the region you're visiting. Locals appreciate when visitors make an effort to speak the local language. Here are some basic phrases in English and Greek that you may find helpful before visiting Cyprus:

Hello - Γεια σας (Gia sas)

Goodbye - Αντίο (Antío)

Please - Παρακαλώ (Parakaló)

Thank you - Ευχαριστώ (Efcharistó)

Yes - Ναι (Nai)

No - Όχι (Ochi)

Excuse me - Συγγνώμη (Syngnómi)

Do you speak English? - Μιλάτε αγγλικά; (Miláte angliká?)

How much does it cost? - Πόσο κοστίζει; (Póso kostízei?)

Where is the restroom? - Πού είναι η τουαλέτα; (Pou íne i toualéta?)

- **Research local customs and etiquette**: Cypriots have a unique culture and customs that visitors should be aware of, such as the importance of hospitality, religious festivals, and mealtime traditions. Researching local customs and etiquette before your trip can help you better understand and appreciate the Cypriot way of life.

By following these tips, you can ensure that your trip to Cyprus is a memorable and enjoyable experience.

How To Get To Cyprus

Cyprus is an island country in the eastern Mediterranean, so the primary way to get there is by air or sea.

By Air:

Cyprus operates with two international airports, Larnaca International Airport and Paphos International Airport. Both airports are well-connected to major cities in Europe, the Middle East, and Asia. You can fly to Cyprus from most major airports around the world, and several airlines offer direct flights to Cyprus. Some of the major airlines that fly to Cyprus include

Cyprus Airways, British Airways, Ryanair, EasyJet, Lufthansa, and Turkish Airlines.

By Sea:

You can also get to Cyprus by ferry from Greece, Turkey, and Israel. There are regular ferry services between Cyprus and Piraeus (Athens), Rhodes, and Crete in Greece, Mersin and Antalya in Turkey, and Haifa in Israel. The ferries are usually large and comfortable, and the journey times vary depending on your departure point.

Once you arrive in Cyprus, you can get around the country by car, taxi, bus, or bicycle. Car rental is a popular option for tourists, but you can also use public transportation to explore the island. Buses are the most common mode of public transportation, and there are frequent services between major cities and towns in Cyprus.

Visa Requirement

Cyprus has a visa policy that varies depending on the nationality of the traveler. Here is some general information about the visa requirements for Cyprus:

- Visa-Free Countries: Citizens of the European Union (EU) member states, the European Economic Area (EEA), and Switzerland do not need a visa to enter Cyprus. Additionally, citizens of many countries, including the United States, Canada, Australia, and New Zealand, can enter Cyprus visa-free for up to 90 days within a 180-day period.

- Visa-on-Arrival: Citizens of some countries, including Russia, India, and China, can obtain a visa-on-arrival when they arrive in Cyprus. This type of visa is valid for up to 90 days and costs €60.
- Visa Required: Citizens of some countries, including Nigeria, Pakistan, and Bangladesh, must apply for a visa before they travel to Cyprus. The visa application process usually takes a few weeks, and applicants must provide proof of accommodation, sufficient funds, and a return ticket.

It is important to note that the visa requirements for Cyprus can change, so it is recommended that travelers check with the Cyprus embassy or consulate in their home country before they travel. Additionally, all visitors to Cyprus must have a valid passport with at least six months' validity remaining.

Currency and Exchange Rate

Cyprus uses Euro (EUR) as their official currency. One euro is divided into 100 cents. As of March 28th, 2023, the exchange rate of the euro to US dollars (USD) is approximately 1 EUR = 1.14 USD.

It's important to note that Cyprus is a popular tourist destination, and many hotels, restaurants, and shops accept major credit cards, such as Visa and Mastercard. ATMs are also widely available in cities and towns across the country, allowing you to withdraw euros using your debit or credit card.

When exchanging money, it's a good idea to compare exchange rates at different banks or currency exchange offices to get the best deal. Banks in Cyprus generally offer competitive exchange rates, but they may charge a commission or transaction fee. Some currency exchange offices may also charge higher fees or offer lower exchange rates, so it's important to check before exchanging money.

Overall, while it is recommended to have some euros on hand when traveling to Cyprus, credit cards and ATMs are widely accepted, making it easy to access cash if needed.

Health and Safety Tips

Cyprus is generally considered a safe destination for travelers, with a low crime rate and a well-established healthcare system. However, it is still important to take some basic health and safety precautions when visiting Cyprus:

- Stay Hydrated: Cyprus has a hot and sunny climate, especially during the summer months, so it's important to drink plenty of water to stay hydrated. You should also avoid spending too much time in the sun, especially during the hottest part of the day.

- Protect Yourself from the Sun: When spending time outdoors, it's important to wear sunscreen, a hat, and sunglasses to protect yourself from the sun's harmful rays. This is especially important for those with fair skin or a history of skin cancer.

- Watch Out for Sea Creatures: If you plan to swim or snorkel in the sea, be aware of jellyfish, sea urchins, and other sea creatures that can cause injury or irritation. If you are stung or injured by a sea creature, seek medical attention immediately.

- Follow Traffic Rules: If you plan to drive in Cyprus, remember to drive on the left-hand side of the road, and follow all traffic rules and speed limits. Always wear a seatbelt and avoid driving under the influence of alcohol or drugs.

- Be Aware of Petty Crime: While Cyprus has a low crime rate, petty crime like pickpocketing and theft can still occur, especially in tourist areas. Be aware of your surroundings, keep your valuables in a secure place, and avoid carrying large amounts of cash or jewelry.

- Stay Up-to-Date on Vaccinations: Make sure your routine vaccinations are up-to-date before traveling to Cyprus. Additionally, some travelers may need to get vaccinated against hepatitis A and B, especially if they plan to spend a lot of time outdoors or have close contact with local people.

Overall, if you take these basic health and safety precautions, you can enjoy a safe and enjoyable trip to Cyprus.

ACCOMMODATION

Cyprus offers a wide range of accommodation options to suit different preferences and budgets. Here are some of the most common types of accommodation in Cyprus:

Hotels

Cyprus has many hotels, ranging from budget-friendly options to luxury resorts. Most hotels offer amenities such as swimming pools, restaurants, and 24-hour reception services.

The majority of hotels in Cyprus can be found in the coastal towns of Ayia Napa, Larnaca, Limassol, and Paphos, with a smaller number of hotels located in the capital city of Nicosia and the mountainous Troodos region.

Many of the hotels in Cyprus offer a range of amenities, such as swimming pools, restaurants, bars, and fitness centers. Some hotels also offer spa services, beach access, and water sports activities. The level of luxury and services provided will vary depending on the hotel's star rating and price point.

When choosing a hotel in Cyprus, it is important to consider your budget, preferred location, and the type of experience you are looking for. Some popular options for budget-friendly accommodation include hostels and guesthouses, while luxury travelers may prefer to stay in a five-star resort or boutique hotel.

Overall, Cyprus offers a diverse range of hotels to suit all tastes and budgets, with something for everyone, from families and couples to solo travelers and groups.

here are some details about the popular hotels in Cyprus that I mentioned earlier:

- Four Seasons Hotel - Limassol: This luxurious five-star hotel is located on a sandy beach in Limassol and offers stunning sea views. It features 6 restaurants, 4 swimming pools, a fitness center, spa, and tennis courts. The rooms and suites are exquisitely planned and prepared with cutting edge comforts.

- Amathus Beach Hotel - Limassol: Another five-star hotel in Limassol, the Amathus Beach Hotel boasts a private beach, 5 restaurants, 2 swimming pools, a spa, and tennis courts. The rooms and suites are spacious and offer sea or garden views.

- Anassa Hotel - Polis Chrysochous: This five-star hotel is located in a secluded bay near the Akamas Peninsula, offering a peaceful retreat for guests. It features 4 restaurants, 2 swimming pools, a spa, and tennis courts. The rooms and suites are decorated with local materials and offer sea or garden views.

- Grecian Park Hotel - Ayia Napa: This four-star hotel is located on a hill overlooking the sea, offering panoramic views. It features 4 restaurants, 2 swimming pools, a spa, and tennis courts. The rooms and suites are decorated in a contemporary style and offer sea or inland views.

- Nissi Beach Resort - Ayia Napa: This four-star hotel is located on the popular Nissi Beach and offers a range of activities, including water sports and beach volleyball. It features 3 restaurants, 2 swimming pools, a spa, and tennis courts. The rooms and suites are spacious and offer garden or sea views.

- Almyra Hotel - Paphos: This four-star hotel is located near the Paphos harbor and offers views of the Mediterranean Sea. It features 4 restaurants, 4 swimming pools, a spa, and tennis courts. The rooms and suites are decorated in a minimalist style and offer garden or sea views.

- Coral Beach Hotel & Resort - Paphos: This five-star hotel is located on a private beach near the Akamas Peninsula and offers stunning sea views. It features 5 restaurants, 2 swimming pools, a spa, and tennis courts. The rooms and suites are spacious and offer sea or garden views.

- St. Raphael Resort - Limassol: This four-star hotel is located on a sandy beach in Limassol and offers views of the Mediterranean Sea. It features 5 restaurants, 2 swimming pools, a spa, and tennis courts. The rooms and suites are decorated in a modern style and offer garden or sea views.

- Columbia Beach Resort - Pissouri: This five-star resort is located on a Blue Flag beach in Pissouri Bay and offers views of the Mediterranean Sea. It features 4 restaurants, 2 swimming pools, a spa, and tennis courts. The rooms and suites are decorated in a traditional style and offer garden or sea views.

- Elysium Hotel - Paphos: This five-star hotel is located on a beach in Paphos and offers views of the Mediterranean Sea. It features 4 restaurants, 2 swimming pools, a spa, and tennis courts. The rooms and suites are elegantly designed and offer garden or sea views.

Villas and Apartments

For those looking for more space and privacy, villas and apartments are a popular choice. These can range from simple apartments to luxurious villas with private pools and other amenities.

Villas in Cyprus are typically spacious, luxurious properties that are located in some of the most beautiful areas of the country. They usually come with a private pool and garden, and can offer stunning views of the sea or the mountains. Some villas in Cyprus are also equipped with modern amenities such as home cinema systems, game rooms, and fully-equipped kitchens.

Apartments in Cyprus are also widely available and offer a more affordable option for travelers who prefer a smaller and more intimate space. Apartments can range from small studio units to larger multi-bedroom apartments that can accommodate families or groups of friends. Most apartments in Cyprus come with modern amenities such as air conditioning, Wi-Fi, and fully-equipped kitchens.

There are many different types of villas and apartments available in Cyprus, ranging from budget-friendly options to luxurious and extravagant properties. Here are some of the most common types of villas and apartments in Cyprus:

- Traditional villas: These are villas that have been built in the traditional Cypriot style, using local materials and incorporating traditional features such as courtyards, terraces, and gardens. These villas offer a unique and authentic experience of Cypriot culture and architecture.

- Modern villas: These are villas that have been built in a more contemporary style, often with sleek and minimalist designs. They may offer cutting-edge amenities such as smart home technology, infinity pools, and outdoor entertainment areas.

- Beachfront villas: These are villas that are located directly on the beach or within walking distance of the sea. They offer stunning views of the Mediterranean and easy access to the beach and water sports activities.

- Golf villas: These are villas that are located near golf courses, offering convenient access to golfing facilities and a tranquil and scenic environment.

- Studio apartments: These are small apartments that typically consist of a single room that serves as the living room, bedroom, and kitchenette. They are suitable for solo travelers or couples who are looking for a budget-friendly option.

When it comes to choosing between a villa or an apartment in Cyprus, it really depends on your personal preferences, travel needs, and budget. If you are traveling with a large group of people or with your family, a villa might be a better option as it can offer more space and privacy. On the other hand, if you are traveling solo or with a smaller group of people, an apartment might be more convenient and budget-friendly.

Overall, both villas and apartments in Cyprus can offer a comfortable and enjoyable stay for visitors. Whether you choose a luxurious villa or a cozy apartment, you can be sure that you will be able to enjoy all that this beautiful country has to offer.

Hostels

Hostels are a budget-friendly option for travelers who don't mind sharing a room with other travelers. Hostels in Cyprus often have shared kitchen facilities, common areas, and activities for guests.

- Location: Hostels in Cyprus can be found in popular tourist destinations such as Ayia Napa, Limassol, Paphos, Larnaca, and Nicosia. Most are located in or near the city center, allowing easy access to local attractions, restaurants, and transportation.

- Price: Hostels in Cyprus are generally cheaper than hotels or private apartments. Prices range from around €10-30 per night, depending on the location, time of year, and the level of amenities provided.

- Amenities: Hostels in Cyprus typically offer basic amenities, including shared dormitory-style rooms or private rooms, communal bathrooms, and shared kitchen facilities. Some may also offer free Wi-Fi, laundry facilities, and common areas for socializing.

- Atmosphere: Hostels in Cyprus attract a diverse range of travelers, including backpackers, students, and budget-conscious tourists. Many hostels offer social events, such as pub crawls or movie nights, to help guests connect with one another.

CHAPTER 2

GETTING AROUND CYPRUS

Cyprus has a relatively good transportation network, with a variety of options available for getting around the island.

Public transportation

Cyprus has a public transportation system consisting of buses, which are relatively cheap and frequent, although they can be quite slow. There are two types of buses - intercity and urban. Intercity buses connect major cities and towns, while urban buses operate within the city and suburban areas. You can purchase tickets on board, but it is cheaper to buy them in advance.

Taxis

Taxis are widely available in Cyprus and are relatively affordable compared to other

European countries. Taxis can be hailed on the street, or you can book one through an app or by calling a taxi company.

Car Rental

Renting a car is a popular option for tourists who want to explore Cyprus on their own. There are several car rental companies operating on the island, and prices are competitive. However, you need to be over 25 years old to rent a car in Cyprus and have a valid driver's license.

Bicycle

Cycling is a great way to explore the island's scenic landscapes, and there are many rental companies in the main tourist areas. However,

Cyprus can be quite hilly, so cycling may not be suitable for everyone.

Walking

Walking is a great way to explore the island's towns and villages. The cities and towns in Cyprus are relatively compact, and most of the main attractions are within walking distance of each other.

Ferries

Ferries are available for travel between Cyprus and other Mediterranean countries such as Greece, Turkey, and Israel. There are also ferry services available for intercity travel within Cyprus, such as from Larnaca to Limassol or from Paphos to Limassol.

Overall, the best way to get around Cyprus depends on your preferences and the purpose of your visit. If you're visiting for a short period and want to explore the main attractions, using public transport or a taxi might be the most convenient option. However, if you want to explore the island more extensively, renting a car or a bicycle would be a better choice.

CHAPTER 3

EXPLORING CYPRUS

Cyprus is a beautiful island country located in the Eastern Mediterranean Sea, known for its crystal-clear waters, golden beaches, picturesque villages, ancient ruins, and rich history. Exploring Cyprus can be a truly unforgettable experience as the island offers a wide range of activities and attractions that cater to different interests and preferences.

One of the most popular tourist destinations in Cyprus is the city of Paphos, which is known for its stunning beaches, ancient ruins, and vibrant nightlife. Visitors can explore the UNESCO World Heritage Site of the Tombs of the Kings, the ancient city of Kourion, and the Paphos

Archaeological Park, which is home to some of the foremost well-preserved mosaics in the world.

Another must-visit destination in Cyprus is the capital city of Nicosia, which is the only divided capital in Europe. Visitors can explore the historic old town and the Venetian Walls, as well as the Green Line, which separates the Greek and Turkish parts of the city.

If you are a nature lover, you can explore the Troodos Mountains, which offer breathtaking views, hiking trails, and opportunities for skiing in the winter. The Akamas Peninsula is another popular destination for nature lovers, with its stunning beaches, rugged cliffs, and diverse wildlife.

Top tourist destinations in Cyprus

Cyprus is a stunning Mediterranean island country that attracts millions of tourists every year. The island is renowned for its beautiful beaches, crystal-clear waters, rich history, and ancient ruins, making it a popular destination for those seeking a mix of sun, sea, and culture. Here's a description of one of the top tourist destinations in Cyprus:

- Limassol - This coastal city is known for its long stretch of sandy beaches, ancient ruins, and modern shopping malls. It's a popular destination for both visitors and local people alike.

- Paphos - Located on the southwest coast of Cyprus, Paphos is a UNESCO World Heritage Site known for its ancient ruins, including the Tombs of the Kings and the Paphos Archaeological Park.

- Nicosia - As the capital city of Cyprus, Nicosia is the cultural and political center of the island. Visitors can explore the historic Old Town, visit the Cyprus Museum, and walk along the Venetian walls.

- Ayia Napa - Known for its vibrant nightlife and stunning beaches, Ayia Napa is a popular destination for young adults. It's also home to the Cape Greco National Forest Park, a beautiful natural area with hiking trails and stunning sea views.

- Troodos Mountains - This mountain range is located in the center of Cyprus and is a popular destination for nature lovers. Visitors can explore picturesque villages, hike in the forest, and visit the stunning Kykkos Monastery.

Off-the-beaten-path attractions in Cyprus

Cyprus, the land of sun, sea, and ancient mythology, is a treasure trove of off-the-beaten-path attractions waiting to be discovered. As you venture beyond the popular tourist spots, you'll discover hidden gems that will take your breath away.

Let's start with the Kato Lefkara village, tucked away in the Troodos Mountains. This charming village is known for its traditional lace-making and silverwork, but its real charm lies in its winding streets and stone houses adorned with colorful flowers. Take a stroll through the village's narrow alleys, and you'll feel like you've stepped back in time.

Next, head to the abandoned village of Varosha, located in the northern part of Cyprus. Once a thriving resort town, Varosha has been frozen in time since 1974, when it was abandoned during the Turkish invasion. The empty hotels, restaurants, and shops are now surrounded by barbed wire and patrolled by Turkish soldiers, giving the town an eerie and surreal atmosphere.

For a dose of adventure, head to the Akamas Peninsula, located on the western coast of Cyprus. This rugged and wild region is home to secluded coves, hidden beaches, and dramatic cliffs that offer breathtaking views of the Mediterranean Sea. Take a hike along one of the many trails that crisscross the peninsula, and you'll feel like you've discovered a secret paradise.

Here are some other suggestions:

Cape Greco: Located on the southeast coast of Cyprus, Cape Greco is a scenic area with stunning sea cliffs, hidden coves, and natural rock formations. It's a great spot for hiking, swimming, and snorkeling.

St. Hilarion Castle: This medieval castle is located in the Kyrenia Mountains and offers spectacular views of the surrounding area. It's also said to have inspired the castle in Disney's "Snow White and the Seven Dwarfs."

Choirokoitia Neolithic Settlement: This UNESCO World Heritage Site is an ancient village that dates back to 7000 BC. It's one of the best-preserved examples of a prehistoric settlement in the eastern Mediterranean.

Larnaca Salt Lake: This shallow lake is located near the city of Larnaca and is a popular spot for birdwatching. It's also known for its pink flamingos, which flock to the area during the winter months.

Akamas Peninsula: Located on the northwest coast of Cyprus, the Akamas Peninsula is a protected nature reserve with rugged cliffs, hidden coves, and pristine beaches. It's a great place for hiking, swimming and exploring.

Beaches and coastal areas in Cyprus

Imagine the Mediterranean Sea in all its turquoise glory, gently kissing the shores of the island of Cyprus. As you approach the coastline, the sweet scent of salty sea air and blooming flora mingle together in a heady bouquet, beckoning you closer. The sandy beaches stretch for miles, their golden hues glistening under the warm Mediterranean sun. You can hear gentle waves lapping against the shore, creating a soothing melody that lulls you into a sense of tranquility.

As you wander along the coast, you'll discover hidden coves and rocky alcoves that offer a more secluded experience. These hidden gems boast crystal-clear waters that reflect the deep blues of the sky, creating a dazzling contrast against the rugged landscape. The coastal areas are adorned with colorful parasols, cozy beach bars, and bustling promenades, where visitors can indulge in authentic Cypriot cuisine and refreshing cocktails while taking in the stunning views. In the distance, you can see the majestic silhouette of the Troodos Mountains, standing tall and proud against the skyline. The mountains offer a breathtaking backdrop, providing a stark contrast to the serene coastal landscape.

Here are some of the most popular beaches and coastal areas in Cyprus:

- Nissi Beach - located in the resort town of Ayia Napa, Nissi Beach is known for its crystal-clear waters and white sand. It's a popular destination for visitors and locals also.

- Fig Tree Bay - another popular beach in the Ayia Napa area, Fig Tree Bay is known for its picturesque views and calm waters. It's a great place for swimming, snorkeling, and sunbathing.

- Coral Bay - located near the town of Paphos, Coral Bay is a family-friendly beach with shallow waters and plenty of amenities like beach bars, restaurants, and water sports rentals.

- Lara Bay - this secluded beach on the Akamas Peninsula is a popular spot for nature lovers and wildlife enthusiasts. It's known for its pristine waters and the presence of loggerhead sea turtles, which come to the area to lay their eggs.

- Latchi Beach - located on the northwest coast of Cyprus, Latchi Beach is a quiet, unspoiled stretch of coastline with crystal-clear waters and views of the Akamas Peninsula. It's a great spot for swimming, snorkeling, and relaxing.

- Mackenzie Beach - located near the city of Larnaca, Mackenzie Beach is a popular spot for both locals and tourists. It's known for its lively atmosphere, clear waters, and views of Larnaca's famous Salt Lake.

Natural parks and outdoor activities in Cyprus

Cyprus is a natural wonderland, offering visitors an abundance of stunning natural parks and outdoor activities to explore. From rugged coastlines and dramatic mountain ranges to ancient ruins and crystal-clear waters, the island's natural beauty will leave you breathless.

In the Akamas Peninsula National Park, you can immerse yourself in a world of unspoiled wilderness. The rugged coastline is a playground for adventure seekers, who can explore hidden coves, dive into the turquoise waters, and discover hidden treasures in the Blue Lagoon. Hikers can follow trails through the park's dense forests and rugged terrain, enjoying panoramic views of the Mediterranean Sea and the surrounding landscape.

The Troodos Mountains offer a tranquil escape from the hustle and bustle of the coastal towns. Visitors can breathe in the crisp mountain air and admire the stunning vistas, while hiking or mountain biking through pine-scented forests and alpine meadows. In the winter months, the mountains are a popular destination for skiing and snowboarding, offering a unique blend of Mediterranean sunshine and alpine terrain.

At Cape Greco National Forest Park, you can experience the raw power of the sea. This rugged coastal park boasts dramatic cliffs, towering rock formations, and crystal-clear waters teeming with marine life. Adventurers can explore underwater caves and swim through rocky archways, while hikers can follow trails that lead to hidden coves and secluded beaches.

Paphos Archaeological Park is a treasure trove of ancient history, offering visitors a glimpse into the island's rich past. Here, you can wander among the ruins of ancient Roman villas, admire the intricate mosaics that adorn the floors of ancient temples, and explore the medieval castle that overlooks the sea.

Finally, for those who seek the thrill of the open water, Cyprus offers an array of water sports activities. The island's warm Mediterranean waters are perfect for windsurfing, kiteboarding, and paddleboarding, while its clear waters provide a perfect environment for snorkeling and scuba diving.

In Cyprus, natural parks and outdoor activities abound, offering visitors a chance to connect with nature, explore the island's rich history, and experience the thrill of adventure in one of the most beautiful destinations on earth.

Historical and cultural sites in Cyprus

Cyprus is a country with a wealth of historical and cultural sites, ranging from ancient settlements and castles to churches and museums. The Paphos Archaeological Site features well-preserved ruins of a Roman villa, a theater, and intricate mosaics, while the Tombs of the Kings showcases elaborate tombs from the Hellenistic and Roman periods. St. Hilarion Castle, perched on the Kyrenia Mountains, is a medieval castle with a rich history, while Kykkos Monastery boasts impressive frescoes and icons. Choirokoitia is a Neolithic village with fascinating remains dating back to the 7th millennium BCE. Other notable sites include the Hala Sultan Tekke mosque, the Kourion ruins, and various museums and churches throughout the country. Here are some of the most notable sites in Cyprus:

- Kourion: Kourion is an ancient city located on the southwestern coast of Cyprus. The site features well-preserved ruins of a theater, public baths, and an agora (marketplace) dating back to the Roman era.

- Paphos Archaeological Site: Paphos Archaeological Site is a vast complex of ruins located in the coastal city of Paphos. The site includes the remains of a Roman villa, a theater, and a series of intricate mosaics.

- Tombs of the Kings: The Tombs of the Kings is a necropolis located on the outskirts of Paphos. The site features a series of elaborate tombs dating back to the Hellenistic and Roman periods.

- St. Hilarion Castle: St. Hilarion Castle is a medieval castle located on the Kyrenia Mountains. The castle dates back to the 10th century and was used by the Byzantines, Crusaders, and Ottomans.

- Kykkos Monastery: Kykkos Monastery is a historic monastery located in the Troodos Mountains. The monastery dates back to the 11th century and is famous for its impressive frescoes and icons.

- Choirokoitia: Choirokoitia is an ancient settlement located in the Larnaca District. The site features the remains of a Neolithic village dating back to the 7th millennium BCE.

- Hala Sultan Tekke: Hala Sultan Tekke is a mosque located on the shores of Larnaca Salt Lake. The mosque is an important pilgrimage site for Muslims and is believed to have been built in honor of Umm Haram, a companion of the Prophet Muhammad.

These are just a few of the many historical and cultural sites in Cyprus. Visitors to the country can also explore numerous museums, churches, and other landmarks that offer insights into Cyprus's rich history and culture.

Festivals and events in Cyprus

Cyprus has a lively calendar of festivals and events throughout the year. These festivals offer visitors a chance to experience Cyprus's rich culture and traditions. Here are some of the most popular Festivals:

- Limassol Carnival: The Limassol Carnival is a 10-day festival that takes place in February or March, just before Lent. The festival features colorful parades, music, dancing, and street performances, and culminates with the burning of a giant effigy of King Carnival.

- Flower Festival: The Flower Festival takes place in May and celebrates the arrival of spring. The festival features parades of flower-decorated floats, music, dancing, and other activities, and takes place in several cities across the island.

- Kataklysmos (Festival of the Flood): Kataklysmos is a popular festival that takes place in June, celebrating the Holy Spirit and the flood of Noah's Ark. The festival features traditional music, dancing, boat races, and other activities, and takes place in various seaside towns and cities.

- Shakespearean Festival: The Shakespearean Festival takes place in July and August, featuring outdoor performances of classic Shakespeare plays in various venues across the island.

- Wine Festivals: Several wine festivals take place in August and September, celebrating Cyprus's rich wine-making heritage. The festivals feature wine tastings, traditional food, music, and other activities, and take place in various cities and villages.

- Ayia Napa Medieval Festival: The Ayia Napa Medieval Festival takes place in October, transporting visitors back in time to the medieval era with reenactments, jousting, live music, and other activities.

- Christmas and New Year's Eve Celebrations: Cyprus celebrates Christmas and New Year's Eve with traditional decorations, music, and food. Cities and towns across the island host events, concerts, and firework displays to ring in the new year.

These festivals and events are just a small sample of the many celebrations that take place throughout the year in Cyprus, showcasing the country's rich culture and traditions.

CHAPTER 4

FOOD AND DRINK IN CYPRUS

Imagine the sun-drenched island of Cyprus as a gastronomic playground, where flavors from the Mediterranean, the Middle East, and beyond come together to create a truly unique culinary experience. Here, your taste buds will be tantalized by a plethora of traditional dishes, bursting with fragrant herbs and spices.

Picture yourself savoring a succulent Souvla, with tender pieces of lamb or pork that have been slow-roasted to perfection over an open charcoal fire. Or perhaps you're indulging in a meze, a never-ending parade of small plates featuring grilled meats, fresh salads, and creamy dips like tzatziki and hummus. The velvety smooth texture of grilled Halloumi cheese, a local specialty, will linger on your palate long after the last bite.

Wash it all down with a glass of Cyprus wine, made from ancient grape varieties that have been cultivated on the island for thousands of years. Sample the crisp and refreshing Xynisteri white wine, or the rich and full-bodied Maratheftiko red wine. And don't forget to try the sweet and velvety Commandaria, one of the oldest wines in the world, made from sun-dried grapes. And if you're in the mood for something sweet, you won't be disappointed. Loukoumades, deep-fried dough balls drizzled with honey syrup, are a heavenly treat. Or indulge in a slice of baklava, layers of crispy phyllo pastry filled with nuts and honey.

Whether you're savoring the flavors of Cyprus at a traditional taverna, a chic café, or a bustling street market, you'll find that the food and drink of this island nation are as rich and diverse as its history and culture. Some of the most popular Cypriot dishes include:

- Meze: A selection of small dishes that are meant to be shared, similar to Spanish tapas. It includes grilled meat, fish, vegetables, dips, and salads.

- Souvla: A traditional Cypriot dish consisting of large pieces of meat (usually lamb or pork) that are slow-roasted on a skewer over an open charcoal fire.

- Kleftiko: A dish made with slow-cooked lamb or goat that is marinated in herbs and spices and then wrapped in parchment paper or foil and baked in a traditional oven.

- Halloumi: A semi-hard cheese made from sheep's and goat's milk that is often grilled or fried and served as a meze or a main course.

- Tzatziki: A dip made with yogurt, cucumber, garlic, and olive oil that is often served as a side dish or a meze.

- Kolokasi: A traditional Cypriot dish made with taro root, which is boiled and then sautéed with garlic, onions, and tomatoes.

- Loukoumades: A popular Cypriot dessert made of small dough balls that are deep-fried and then drizzled with honey syrup.

In addition to wine, Cyprus is also known for its coffee culture, with traditional coffeehouses (known as kafeneio) serving strong, dark coffee and sweet treats like loukoumades and baklava.

CHAPTER 5

SHOPPING IN CYPRUS

Shopping in Cyprus can be a fun and rewarding experience, with a variety of options to suit different tastes and budgets. Whether you're looking for local crafts and souvenirs, designer fashion, or everyday essentials, you'll find plenty of options to choose from.

One of the most popular shopping destinations in Cyprus is the capital city of Nicosia, where you can explore the narrow streets of the old town and discover artisanal shops selling handmade pottery, jewelry, and textiles.

You can also visit the Ledra Street shopping district, where you'll find a mix of international brands, department stores, and local boutiques.

Another great place to shop in Cyprus is the coastal city of Limassol, where you'll find a wide range of options from high-end fashion to local produce. The Limassol Marina is a popular spot for luxury shopping, with a selection of high-end fashion brands, while the Limassol Old Town is a great place to explore local crafts and antiques.

If you're looking for a more traditional shopping experience, you can visit the local markets, or 'agoras,' that can be found in most towns and cities in Cyprus. Here, you can haggle for fresh produce, spices, and souvenirs, and immerse yourself in the local culture.

For those looking for modern shopping malls, there are several options available in Cyprus, including the Mall of Cyprus in Nicosia, the Kings Avenue Mall in Paphos, and the MyMall Limassol.

Overall, shopping in Cyprus offers a unique blend of local and international products, allowing visitors to experience the best of both worlds while enjoying the island's rich culture and hospitality.

CHAPTER 6

NIGHTLIFE IN CYPRUS

Cyprus has a vibrant and diverse nightlife scene, with something to suit every taste and preference. Whether you're looking for a quiet drink at a local tavern or an all-night party at a club, you'll find plenty of options to choose from.

The island's most popular nightlife destinations are located in the coastal cities of Limassol, Ayia Napa, and Paphos. Ayia Napa, in particular, is known for its lively and energetic nightlife, with an abundance of bars, clubs, and beach parties that attract a young and party-loving crowd.

Limassol also offers a wide range of nightlife options, with a mix of sophisticated rooftop bars, beach clubs, and music venues that cater to a more mature and upscale crowd. Paphos, on the other hand, has a more relaxed and laid-back atmosphere, with plenty of cozy bars and pubs that are perfect for a quiet night out.

In addition to the traditional bar and club scene, Cyprus also offers a range of cultural and entertainment events, including theater performances, concerts, and festivals. The Kourion Ancient Amphitheater in Limassol is a popular venue for concerts and other cultural events, while the Limassol Wine Festival and the Pafos Aphrodite Festival attract thousands of visitors each year.

That been said, the nightlife in Cyprus is diverse, exciting, and welcoming to visitors from all walks of life. Whether you're looking for a wild night out or a more laid-back experience, Cyprus has something to offer everyone.

Bars and clubs in Cyprus

Cyprus is home to a variety of bars and clubs, each offering a unique experience. Here are some of the top bars and clubs in Cyprus:

- Castle Club, Ayia Napa: This multi-level club is one of the largest in Cyprus and attracts thousands of visitors every year. It features several dance floors, a VIP area, and a pool bar, making it a popular destination for party-goers.

- Guaba Beach Bar, Limassol: Located on the beach, Guaba Beach Bar is a popular spot for daytime and nighttime parties. It features a large dance floor, a stage for live music and performances, and stunning views of the sea.

- Havana Club, Paphos: This Latin-inspired club in Paphos is a popular destination for salsa dancing and live music. It features a spacious dance floor, a VIP area, and a terrace with sea views.

- Sinners, Ayia Napa: This club is known for its wild and energetic atmosphere, with resident DJs playing a mix of house, techno, and trance music. It features several bars, a dance floor, and a rooftop terrace.

- The Irish Pub, Limassol: This traditional Irish pub in Limassol is a popular spot for a more laid-back night out. It features live music, a large selection of drinks, and a cozy atmosphere.

- Sky Bar, Nicosia: Located on the rooftop of a hotel in Nicosia, Sky Bar offers stunning views of the city and a sophisticated atmosphere. It features a cocktail bar, a lounge area, and live music events.

Generally, Cyprus offers a wide range of bars and clubs to suit different preferences and budgets. Whether you're looking for a wild night out or a more relaxed experience, you'll find something to enjoy in Cyprus.

Live music and entertainment in Cyprus

Cyprus has a vibrant live music and entertainment scene, with a range of venues and events to suit different tastes and preferences.

Here are some of the top live music and entertainment destinations in Cyprus:

- Kourion Ancient Amphitheatre, Limassol: This ancient amphitheater is a popular venue for live music concerts, theater performances, and other cultural events. It offers stunning views of the Mediterranean and can seat up to 3,500 people.

- Rialto Theatre, Limassol: This modern theater in Limassol hosts a range of cultural events, including theater performances, concerts, and film screenings. It has a capacity of 550 people and features state-of-the-art sound and lighting systems.

- Pafos Aphrodite Festival, Paphos: This annual festival celebrates the arts and culture of Cyprus and attracts thousands of visitors each year. It features opera performances, theater shows, and live music concerts.

- Savino Live, Larnaca: This music venue in Larnaca is a popular destination for live music events, with a focus on rock, metal, and blues music. It features a bar, a dance floor, and a stage for live performances.

- Red Music Stage, Nicosia: This music venue in Nicosia is a popular spot for local and international bands, with a focus on alternative and indie music. It features a bar, a dance floor, and a stage for live performances.

Cyprus has a diverse live music and entertainment scene that caters to a range of tastes and preferences. Whether you're interested in theater, opera, or live music, you'll find plenty of options to enjoy in Cyprus.

Casinos in Cyprus

Cyprus is home to several casinos, offering a range of games and entertainment options. Here are some of the top casinos in Cyprus:

City of Dreams Mediterranean, Limassol: This luxury casino and resort is one of the largest in Europe, with over 1,200 slot machines and 140 gaming tables. It also features several restaurants, bars, and a hotel.

C2 - Cyprus Casinos, Nicosia: This casino in the capital city offers a range of games, including slot machines, blackjack, and roulette. It also features a sports bar, a restaurant, and a VIP gaming area.

Merit Crystal Cove Hotel & Casino, Kyrenia: This casino is located on the northern side of Cyprus, and it features several gaming options, including slot machines and table games. It also has a hotel, spa, and several restaurants.

Olympic Casino, Larnaca: This casino in Larnaca offers a range of slot machines and table games, including blackjack and roulette. There is also a sports bar and a restaurant.

Liman Casino, Kyrenia: This casino is located in a historic castle in Kyrenia and offers a range of slot machines and table games. It also features several restaurants and bars.

Cyprus offers several options for those who enjoy casinos and gambling, with a range of games and entertainment options available. However, it's important to remember to gamble responsibly and within your means.

CONCLUSION

In conclusion, Cyprus is a stunning Mediterranean island that offers a diverse range of experiences for travelers. From ancient ruins and traditional villages to beautiful beaches and vibrant nightlife, there's something for everyone to enjoy. With its delicious cuisine, friendly locals, and rich cultural heritage, Cyprus is a destination that is sure to leave a lasting impression. By following the practical information and recommendations provided in this travel guide, visitors can have a safe and enjoyable trip to this beautiful island.

Expert tips and recommendations for travellers to Cyprus

Here are some expert tips and recommendations for travellers to Cyprus:

- Rent a car: Renting a car in Cyprus is a great way to explore the island at your own pace. Just be aware that driving is on the left side of the road.

- Try local delicacies: Cyprus has a unique cuisine that is influenced by both Greek and Turkish cultures. Don't be afraid to try local delicacies such as halloumi cheese, loukoumades, and souvlaki.

- Visit during the shoulder season: Summer is the peak season in Cyprus, with higher prices and crowds. Consider visiting during the shoulder season (May-June or

September-October) for milder weather and fewer crowds.

- Respect local customs: Cyprus has a rich cultural heritage, and visitors are encouraged to respect local customs and traditions. Dress appropriately when visiting religious sites, and be aware of social customs such as greeting people with a handshake or kiss on the cheek.

- Explore beyond the beaches: While Cyprus is known for its beautiful beaches, there's much more to explore. Don't miss the Troodos Mountains, traditional villages, and ancient ruins.

- Stay hydrated: Cyprus can get very hot in the summer, so it's important to stay hydrated. Bring a refillable water bottle to stay hydrated throughout the day.

- Be mindful of the environment: Cyprus is a beautiful island, and it's important to help keep it that way. Respect the environment by not littering, conserving water, and following local recycling guidelines.

By keeping these tips in mind, you can have a safe, enjoyable, and respectful trip to Cyprus.

Printed in Great Britain
by Amazon